# Contents

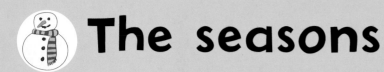

# The seasons

There are four seasons in the year. The seasons are called spring, summer, autumn and winter. Each season is different.

4

# Winter

Kay Barnham

WAYLAND

# Explore the world with **Popcorn** - your complete first non-fiction library.

Look out for more titles in the **Popcorn** range. All books have the same format of simple text and awesome images. Text is carefully matched to the pictures to help readers to identify and understand key vocabulary.
www.waylandbooks.co.uk/popcorn

First published in 2009 by Wayland
First published in paperback in 2011
Copyright © Wayland 2009

Wayland
Hachette Children's Books
338 Euston Road
London NW1 3BH

Wayland Australia
Level 17/207 Kent Street
Sydney NSW 2000

Senior Editor: Claire Shanahan
Designer: Ruth Cowan
Picture Researcher: Louise Edgeworth
Concept Designer: Paul Cherrill

British Library Cataloguing in Publication Data:
Barnham, Kay
Winter. - (Popcorn. Seasons ; v. 1)
1. Winter - Juvenile literature
I. Title
508.2

ISBN: 978 07502 6668 0

Printed and bound in China

Wayland is a division of Hachette Children's Books,
an Hachette UK Company.
www.hachette.co.uk

Acknowledgements:
Alamy: Tim Graham p8, Renee Morris p10, Blinkwinkel p12, Arco Images GmbH p13, Mike Booth p14, Workingwales p16, View Stock p19; Corbis Images: Ariel Skelley p7 and COVER, Herbert Spichtinger/zefa p9, Creasource p18; Getty Images: David Cavagnaro Imprint page, Tim Graham p4-5, David Cavagnaro p11; iStockphoto: Michele Galli Title page, Jason Lugo p6, Michele Galli p15, Alan Egginton p17.

In winter, the nights are long and the days are short. The winter months are December, January and February.

# Winter weather

The weather is often very cold in winter.

It may be wet and windy.

Winter is the
coldest season
of the year.

Sometimes, it is so cold that snow falls. Snow is lots of small flakes of frozen water.

Building a snowman in winter is fun !

# Winter trees

Many trees lose their leaves in autumn.
By winter, their branches and twigs are
bare. In spring, new leaves will grow.

This robin is
easy to spot
among the
bare
branches.

Some trees keep their leaves all year round. These trees are called evergreens.

Evergreen trees always have green leaves, even in winter.

# Winter plants

Most plants stop growing in winter. This helps them to survive the cold weather. But a few plants, such as holly and mistletoe, do grow.

In winter, birds feed on holly berries.

Snowdrops are small, white flowers. They are tough enough to survive the cold even when there is snow on the ground!

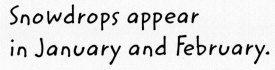

Snowdrops appear in January and February.

# Animals in winter

In winter, it is hard for animals to survive. Many of them go to sleep until warmer weather comes. This sleep is called hibernation.

Hibernating bears can survive without food or water for three months or more!

Some birds fly to hot countries.
This journey is called migration.
They will come back when winter
is over.

Arctic Terns fly futher than any other
bird to reach warmer weather.

# Winter fun

There are lots of winter sports to enjoy. Why not learn to ice-skate? If there is a little snow, you can try sledging, too.

Ice-skaters whizz across the ice on narrow blades.

In some countries, lots of snow falls in winter. Skiers and snowboarders zoom down snowy mountains.

Many people spend winter holidays skiing or snowboarding.

# Winter food

In winter, there is lots of delicious food to eat. Brussels sprouts, cabbages, parsnips and leeks are all ready to be harvested.

Look out for fresh winter vegetables in markets.

Hot food helps to keep us warm in winter. Vegetables can be made into hearty soups and stews.

Hot soup is the perfect meal for a cold day.

# Winter festivals

There are many festivals during winter.
Christmas Day is on 25 December.
It is the birthday of Jesus Christ.

Many people
celebrate
Christmas
by giving
presents.

Chinese New Year happens in January or February. It is the most important of all Chinese holidays.

At Chinese New Year, people wish each other luck for the new year.

# Why do we have seasons?

We have seasons because Earth is tilted. As Earth moves around the Sun, different parts of the planet are nearer the Sun.

In **spring**, our part of the planet moves towards the Sun. The weather grows warmer.

In **summer**, our part of the planet is nearest the Sun. This means that the weather is hot.

In **autumn**, our part of the planet moves away from the Sun. The weather grows cooler.

In **winter**, our part of the planet is furthest from the Sun. This means that the weather is cold.

It takes a year for the four seasons to happen. This is because it takes a year for Earth to move around the Sun.

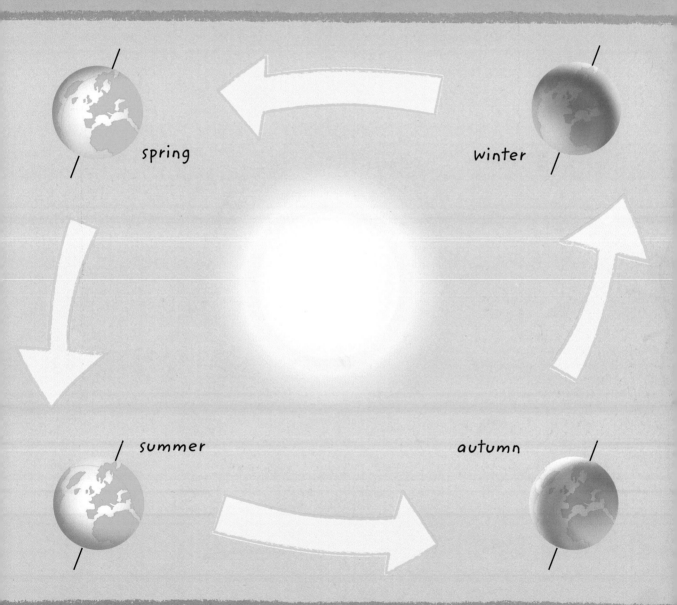

spring

winter

summer

autumn

# Make a snowflake

You will need:
• coloured paper cut into squares
• pencil
• scissors

Snowflakes make lovely decorations. You can make your very own paper snowflake by following these simple instructions.

1. Fold the paper in half from one corner to the opposite corner. This will make a triangle.

2. Fold the paper in half again, from the top corner to the bottom right corner. This will make a smaller triangle.

3. Now fold the left corner in and then the right corner in. The shape you'll make is below on the right.

4. Cut off the jagged end at the bottom to make a straight edge. Be careful with the scissors!

5. Make tiny cuts into the sides of the triangle.

6. When you open up the triangle, you'll have a snowflake decoration unlike any other! Hang it up or stick it on a window.

# Glossary

**Arctic tern** a seabird that comes from northern parts of the world

**evergreen** a tree or plant that has green leaves all year round

**harvested** when fruit, vegetables or crops are picked

**hearty** wholesome, tasty and filling

**hibernation** when animals sleep for a long time in cold weather

**holly** a plant that has dark green, prickly leaves and red berries in winter

**Jesus Christ** the person who started the Christian religion

**migration** when animals travel to warmer countries in cold weather

**mistletoe** a plant that has white berries in winter

# Index